Looking for Scotland

poems by

Sally Evans

UNIVERSITY OF SALZBURG

First published in 1996 by Salzburg University in its series:

SALZBURG STUDIES IN ENGLISH LITERATURE
POETIC DRAMA & POETIC THEORY
187

Editors: Wolfgang Görtschacher & James Hogg

Copyright © Sally Evans 1996

ISBN: 3-7052-0053-4

INSTITUT FÜR ANGLISTIK UND AMERIKANISTIK
UNIVERSITÄT SALZBURG
A-5020 SALZBURG
AUSTRIA

SALZBURG - OXFORD - PORTLAND

Distributed by DRAKE INTERNATIONAL SERVICES
Market House, Market Place,
Deddington
OXFORD OX15 0SF
Tel. 01869 338240

Contents

Introduction

Sally Evans' work will seem quirky and idiosyncratic to some. I hope so, because that is something in its favour. That is what is so refreshing and– dare I say it?– so cheeky about it.

That slanted view which seems not to be taking her subjects so seriously – and yet is in its way – is not just idiosyncratic. It has a touch of uniqueness about it which, I believe, is the hallmark of all authentic creation.

Every poet has their particular forte, things they should develop (perhaps) at the expense of others, because that is where their true strengths lie. As long as they do that, they will not be selling us short because they will be giving us the pith of themselves. Others may say, "Oh look, she hasn't done this, or hasn't attended to this as she should." Perhaps, they will accuse her of being maladroit here and there, without stopping to consider whether this was part of the plan – like the clown who lands on his buttocks (That's an art!). Evans' work appears maladroit in places, especially the wonderful *Fishing in Gairloch*, but when you see what she is actually doing, you will also see that appearances can be deceptive.

Reading this book one cannot help but gain an impression of the richness of imagination which has gone into its composition. This is the background against which you must judge her 'idiosyncrasies'.

Sally Evans is clearly a seasoned poet who, in terms of the imagination, has gone into the world to collect her material and bring it back into her work, as in *Yew Hedge* for instance: "envy the rampant vine / bolting up the yard fence, snatching a telegraph pole / out of its asphalt forest floor." Observation is apparent everywhere, but it is more than just observation. There is some kind of vision in the detailed presentation which it is hard to ignore.

Many poets beaver away, and because their work does not conform to prevailing fashions, they largely go unnoticed. This is more often due to a surplus of personality rather than a lack. Trim your sails (or have no sails!) and you may get noticed. What I admire about Sally Evans' work is that it will have none of this. She ignores prevailing currents and trends in order to bring back something much more worth having. A new and unique way of seeing the world. And there can hardly be a higher recommendation than that.

Richard Livermore
Edinburgh, 1996

"The essence of art is we are not very good at it."

– *Miroslav Holub*

for Ian and Robin

Every Summertime

We slept on light at the head of the glen,
our eyes closed on mountain, loch and island.
Our ears heard the dawn bleating of huffy sheep
in whose path we lay. It never got dark
but a landrover with search-lights
crawled down the glen, playing with its beam,
sending wobbly ovals of gold onto the green braes
and silver onto the pale drifts of purple.

We drank peaty highland water
and picnicked from a car, well versed
left nothing behind but happiness,
peeled off a layer of memory to hug
in the generous air. Skimmed down that favourite
incline in low gear and alone, but for the stare
of a still deer, the foolishness of a few rabbits.

But round the corner of a tiny waterfall
I found a wall of violets in moss
later and purpler than believable.
Them I took with me. The smallness of detail
on the vast plain, one concept
I carried over ferries purely as mine.

We do not dine indoors. We are country people
who have to be up on the hills every summertime.

New Poem

I do not want to give you my poem yet.
I want to own it just a little longer.
I want to look at it while the ink's wet
and it still shines with the beauty of where it came from:
tomorrow it may be dusty, or an old toy
with cracks in the construction; today, it thrills
and I do not want to give it away.

I do not want to write another poem,
I still love this one. I fidgeted with words,
rhymed a few concepts, spoke to the birds
who cawed or chirruped, whichever suited them
or said, "Really", "Hello dear", or "hem hem"
but not one of them gave me a real song.
They went back to laughing in the trees
I could not copy onto my paper.

So I went back to my other poem (the one
I do not want to give you) and said, "Yes,
I still love you" and suddenly the sun
burst out of hiding and lit up the world
dressed, in that instant, in my very words,
and after that I could discard the poem,
                    like a cloak
or, much more probably, a caul.
It's birth we are concerned with, after all.

Saint Kentigern

Ireland began with the saints,
    and the saints were habitual leaders,
spirited malcontents,
    our earliest writers and readers.
Britain even then
    believed it was lost, in a limbo,
landmass surrounded by foam,
    dispersed in the gloomiest forest.

Britain had one great asset,
    its western physical harbours,
lochs, rivers, estuaries, bays
    waiting for word-bringing settlers.
Thither Saint Kentigern
    and his Celtic and Latin brothers,
sea-scouts with sinking tents,
    prospectors rushing for soul-gold.

The sea-waves bobbed with coracles,
strong fragile mobile oracles
like eggshell cradling embryos
until they blossomed out or froze
or, rocked by islands in the Clyde,
grew famous by that riverside.

In the beginning, Saint Kentigern,
a ludicrous and spirited recluse
haunts an unpeopled paradise,
a corner of a glorious land
honoured by strength and struggle leading back
to an unhistoried time before all that.

His enemies have robbed him of his fire
and as he curses them beneath a tree
a green and leafy bough bursts into flame,
crackles, then restores miraculous light.

But in the tree a robin slept: it dies;
and instantly repenting, he restores
life to the bird; a greater power
than he has called upon before.

The robin, shocked, but ultimately unscathed
flies with his incredible story to a bush
beside a salmon pool in which a king
has flung in a rage an incriminating ring.

Again he intervenes: the saint is loth
to leave the weeping queen to the king's wrath.
A fish gasps, landed; the ring is in its mouth.
The ring sparkles; the tree recovers;
the queen is saved; all the light
from her eyes illuminates the place;
the fish, released, unnoticed, slides downstream.

If patron saints have such remarkable effect,
then founding Glasgow, why, is stark
simplicity; the strength and stress
that place imposes has its fount
in streams Saint Mungo dares to count,
so many fill the darksome Clyde,
a silver, shimmering ecosystem
for salmon of the same description.

And when Glaswegian from the ark
or Eden, or from light and dark
first wanders here to find the river
and make nearby his home for ever,
and Kentigern goes staggering south
to tame wet Kendal with an oath
he sits and stares at Windermere
and swears, *I won't found Glasgow here:*
Glaswegians need a link with harshest sea:
around the Clyde let them forever be.

So, on the Clyde the lovely Glasgow stood,
a village freshly built of stone and wood,
a village with a destiny
to stand in for a history
where the great powers of humanity
would be acted out in mud.

Kentigern, or Mungo – they're the same
in the same way that fiddle and violin
meet in a single word – viol, fidol
or perhaps like Ferdinand might become Andy
or – some derivation would be undoubtedly handy
to explain why Mungo and Kentigern were regarded
as the same name. Fish language or tree language
or keen queenly nomenclature
for an artist of a remarkable nature.

And, life begun, with bears and wolves,
wild pigs, stags, boars and kelpies,
boogeys, woodwose, fogeys and elves,
believable or unbelievable,
on hills, round bends of the river,
up foothills and behind farms,
on long fallow stretches and above churchyards,
beside dancehalls and outside cinemas,
Glasgow was getting under way.

Before wars and after depressions,
in rain and drought, hailstorm and blizzard,
in the glare of undetection, or under scrutiny,
brick after brick, piece of rubbish after piece
of rubbish after stone after sword
after boat after bomb after wheel after aeroplane
Glasgow was getting under way.

And on the Clyde the lovely Glasgow stood,
waiting for big orange buses and the West End,
waiting for department stores and commercial houses,
waiting for rubber factories and satellite shipyards,
waiting for tenements and children's games,
for the Botanical Gardens and plants with Latin names,
waiting to abolish human sacrifices and the tawse,
waiting to rehouse the elderly and reform the whores.

    Yet anyone found to be elderly or a whore
        was already a survivor,
    more so than a clapped out fitter
    or a winded deep-sea diver.

Oh Saint Mungo what would you think
of a Glasgow already on yet another brink
Oh Saint Kentigern what would you say
if you could visit Glasgow today,
be shown round the fin de siècle on a bicycle,
shooed away by the traffic wardens
wined and dined by the Provost
scowled at by the Police?

You it was started Glasgow,
the project dearest to your heart,
and one hell of an art-form,
you and Romulus and Remus.
Would you wake up and scream?

No: you would dream and smile.
You would dream and smile, in your park,
up your listed tree, in your city farm,
or your cave, or your vault,
and triumphantly raise your arm,
glad it was all your fault.

On This Paper

On this paper floats a poem,

on the same page, the pattern of a glass

cut in thistles and rondels flutes in the light.

As I turn the stem, stars twirl in the heavens,

witching round the spaces between the sharp

haloed shadow of clear light-coloured glass,

its celebrants dancing over whiteness.

The poem, and the shadow

of the glass

fix

paper,

each

a kind

of photograph,

a future memory of when

my fingers hover with a pen. I'll drink the verse,

and promise to recite the glass.

Shoes from the Sea

Shoes from the rough icy sea,
with voices chanting above,
boots of boys and men,
legions of sandals,
children crying and playing,
girls and men by the sea,
anklet and heel, tide-washed
salted uppers, the time
the tide took to sweep them,
as these shoes' inhabitants
communed with shore and sky.

Who has not walked by the tide
and seen, among seaweed and wood,
a wonderful sea-washed door,
a lost canvas, serviceable?
And who has not seen sleep
in the limpets and grains
a slipper, a woman's shoe,
a plimsoll, always singly?
The partner never comes
for the sea is lonely,
the shoe's owner a ghost
forever walking the sands,
or wading the long tides.

Now, if I see a shoe
by the tideline, I know it anew,
shoe from the rough icy sea
with a voice to speak and cry.

Our Seas

The order of this poem is: Pictures 1 to 19 and then read back (Pictures 20 to 37). You have thus viewed a gallery of pictures, going round the room in one direction and returning in the other.

Pictures 1 and 37
Your seas, more limpid and turquoise than ours,
describe a cool riviera, grass air-laved cliff vale,
in which might surface a philosophic dolphin
with a humanized name; or a beach-obsessed,
tusked, oilskinned clearly untamed walrus;
seas always gazed on, paletted, artist's seas
rising and falling between calibrations
on a black breakwater; wired to a metronome.

Pictures 2 and 36
But our seas are grey, rough, and threatening,
a menace of stretched glen-ending and raised links.
A revolutionary line of seashore pines
falling on the beach, trunks end-on rolling,
rolling from the sand in the battering spray
and catching under the roots of the next rank,
second pine row underpinned with sand
pushing vegetatively waterward, claiming land
from a seaworld that throws up jellyfish, grey hard hats,
fishboxes, flatfish, bits of brown crusty lamina,
sea-fauna or sea-flora or sea-in-between,
greedy anemone or fleshy samphire, brine-plant.

Pictures 3 and 35
When in hot summer weather we dare in the bay
or open-ended loch by the scene-stealing mountains
behold our glancing evening northern lights, dancing
in the vault where a moon rainbow balances the moon
across the unwilling darkness of the small-hour sky
we love our unlimpid unturquoise seas, wherefore we try
in the face of you, warm-sea owners, white cliff,
flowery meadow-headland feuholders, to argue why.

Pictures 4 and 34
It is the shore we speak of more than the sea.
Landlubbers camping on the sparse gamut of rock;
its mineral gifts; we live with what we chose,
a state of cool fruity fruition; little wild apples
and naturalized island pippins and coxes,
strains that will grow true from a pip
in a sandy garden of a fisherman's father-in-law,
and fertilise from crab or blackberry, even,
as the stain of the peach or mauve juice
flows into the torn petal, corona of miniature rose,
apple, thorn apple, blet of medlar, wasps happy
in a riot of fruit flesh, and the sea buckthorn
so like the tamarind or tamarisk.

Pictures 5 and 33
Berries scented and rare and of such colour
only the few old wives know whether to cook
all included in a honey-sweet hedgerow jelly,
the bullace, the slim red barberry grubbed away
from fields for rusting corn, including
the half-red half-green changeling apple; the acorn
tasting of very fresh oasis desert dates;
and what of the floating coconut bobbing
its way to the islands where all else is strange,
hanging in on its natural lifebuoy like a cocacola bottle.

Pictures 6 and 32

The landlubbers down below
are telling very tall stories, pause and listen
for the crash of breakers, the break of crashed tankers.
Alarm has been heard for the life of rockpools,
seals, birds, plants, fish, and shelled worms.
No creature has wholly survived to tell the tale,
though none can speak any other's language,
but it is feared the black sea from the tanker
is to be feared. Trouble is sensed by the humans.
Scientists come down to the beach angry,
journalists come down to the beach on season tickets,
the harbourmen swear and kick the sand
and walk unhappily into their houses.
Children do not come down to the beach.

Pictures 7 and 31

Old people will be charged with pollution crimes
for transgressing international humanism
when all they ever did was fail to care –
haven't we heard this one before somewhere?
and races of limpets went to limpet death.
Not to lack the courage of their convictions,
no, but to have no convictions –
no convictions for bad behaviour
and no convictions about how to behave.

Pictures 8 and 30

All they ever did was nothing.
Nothing to be remembered by,
no one they ever had a punch up with,
no one they ever got on the wrong side of,
nothing they even resented enough
to lift one little finger in defiance,
not one little finger, flick-knife, offensive weapon,
or dagger of conscience, not one shield of remorse.
Nobody ever needed to police them,
their telephone tapper never got promotion,
earth never evinced from them one shred of emotion.

Pictures 9 and 29

Turquoise and black are not the sea's only colours
but they well express the imps and ferocity,
seals, moods, and the sun-blinded blinking glimpse
of the smooth reflecting glistening steel flat
we call millpond, for no apparent reason:
millponds are dirty and adorned with dabchicks
chugging about: but seabirds ride serene –
the waves chugging under them at turn of tide.
Turquoise and black are the two colours on white
of the seaside souvenir booklet from John O'Groats
in the Most Northerly Shop on the Mainland –
stilted off the land, over the beach
and therefore deserving a place in the poem *Our Seas*
(which, as the philosophy teacher would delight
in telling his seminar, is *this* poem).

Pictures 10 and 28

Other things happen in the poem *Our Seas*.
I think in it. I like to think of the thalassophile
my friend in the northern storms of winter,
I like to think of his shiny books
holding out dry in their timber above the raging beach,
fluid rubbery kelp twanging, the need
for the sucking anchor to be stronger than the flag,
barnacles eating other barnacles, razors dug
deeper that the rattling calcinareous topsands,
down where charybdids doze and the mermaids are blind,
deep and safe in a cosy saltpan of slime.

Pictures 11 and 27

Papery books. They are safe in their glassy cabinet, safe
from the freezing gales, the salt and the silence
in the shop with windows to the blue, awaiting
the summer visitors, desired and desirous,
the fauna, those tourists to arrive,
speaking with the tongues of America and France,
Germany, Texas, Rejkjavik and Provence,
going *bitte guys wow bitte bitte pardon*
wandering round the apparent paradise garden,

Pictures 12 and 26

Having chuntered the length of the country in their cars,
all the A1, all the A9, more and more big bridges
till suddenly, in summer, it is growing lighter
as they drive north into the night.
Or they wend round the west, driving glutted
with mountain, seascape, lochscape, and hotels.
Ben Nevis and Stack Polly in the one day,
the huge beaches, roads that become again laughable
after each of those disrupting improvements:
roads crept along in twos by badger and fox, aware
that after dark, great stags parade each thoroughfare.

Pictures 13 and 25

Or having pitched a tiny tent
in the lee of a stone-slab wall on a high cliff.
Or having slept in a broch.
Or having driven all night, driven, driven
till land crossing is almost piloting,
the same sense of animals getting their kill,
the very elements sniggering over the tenderfoot.
A mass of tadpoles pooled above a cataract:
will they become froglets or smithereens,
or will they survive that terrific natural ride,
flumier than flumes, a most dangerous place
for bigger animals – is there hell below
their ratless catless tadpole-nursery heaven?

Pictures 14 and 24

And if as frogs they hop towards the rise,
crossing tarmac that sometimes takes no cars
for a whole week, in winter – and remark,
these frogs know nothing at all about the world
as you and I think of it – what will be their fate?
What will get them? A hawk or an eagle,
a wildcat that isn't hungry, a stray stoat,
a beastly little foxcub, a pothole, a pig,
a precipice, a waterless plateau,
dangers known only by an innate sense
of external hostility, a universe of selfishness
justified by each individual trek towards survival
until something else within that universe
gives it come-uppance by the throat.

Pictures 15 and 23

Unschooled imagination is Science's enemy.
Imagination can work amidships
as an able-seaman; it can sluice bilge,
or eavesdrop in barrels etc., but the officers
have sextants, seniority and computers,
microscopes, scalpels and massive tomes,
encyclopedias on CD, internets in their homes
and radios at the head of their chandlered cabin bunks.
The bread and margarine may be a bit iffy
after so long at sea, but that chamfered table
and the hook to lodge the breakfast tray,
the drain-like porthole inches above the grey,
the choppy nothing of the sea-surface, they're OK.

Pictures 16 and 22

So much is clear, the coast is where
armies led over continents break rank and rejoice
to see the ocean that cannot quench their thirst,
where caps are thrown from crows-nest spires
by long-term sailors approaching seedy ports,
long desired, growing out of a low line of cloud,
the dull boring shape of peopled land,
the houses rows of dice, the quays toytown
till when they actually get there, work dispels
mermaidenly illusions, and the seabord tarts
are more to them than all the imaginative arts.

Pictures 17 and 21

When I say we have different seas I mean
wild people see tempting wild seas
and warm people see warm smooth seas,
crocodiled, or coral-walled, no breeze,
a sea you could put a brown toe in, and swim.
But don't mention such a thing to him,
he survived two days on a lifebelt spar
kept alive only by an orange anorak
till flown by helicopter to a hospital bed.
A lighthouse-keeper sees a memory
of shuddering breakers scattering
ocean-drops the size and weight
of half-gallon cartons, without trying;
a coble fisher foresees his kippers drying.

Pictures 18 and 20

Go down to writing about the seas again,
they are inexhaustible, Homer's and Vergil's
and Lucy Irvine's seas, Scott's and Heyerdahl's,
our own far from humble marine environment,
the certainty that you have particular seas.
No one could be on land that did not gaze on them,
even in tundra or prairie, even the child
who has never seen the sea knows it.
Very few of us live on it. Early peoples on rafts
declared the sea more cultured than barren infested land,
islands of turtles living peaceably and aged,
islands of tigers killing foxes, foxes birds,
birds in variety devouring fish
and fish sometimes getting to poison something
a tiger might by a stretch of credulity eat.

Picture 19

As long as our seas can be seen we are happy enough.
We stray far inland in a single night, yet drive
coast to coast for the better weather, the cooler
or warmer more soothingly desolate sands,
beaches white as shell for cantering down,
shell-white, as lapping waves, the mind an easel,
stipple with their fringed turquoise the foreshore,
blue-black and grey like shining sea-mussels
pretending to be little sailors, like feathers
from eider duck and cormorant, dark, strong,
tidal. Come here. There, in the sand-pool
the hermit crabs change shells.

Sola at Cumae

Napoli (Naples): the skiffs of the rich
sketched by the student plying her crayon
attempting to take home pictures
and yet re-entering
the high floor of the hotel:

Napoli (Naples): the ways of the poor,
rat-runs and vertical layouts,
roofs, balconies, playgrounds, doors.
Heat and melons. Drought and seascapes.
Soldi: the valuable and the voluble.

Capri: a vision from the shore.
Great railroads to Amalfi.
A dull military castle
holds the road round the bay:
a watery crayon drawing.

Napoli (Naples): the stars
and the great stairs to the Museo
its empty halls grand and peopled
only with marble and alabaster
colder and vaster than time.

Vesuvio: the train
Circum-Vesuviano:
rattling and hooting, earthy and fast:
the adventure, going up to the crater
and the return ride, dusty with ash.

Pompeii: the hot dry day,
the hot roads and the fig tree
and eggshell treasures
lifted out of their hollows
by would-be amorous guides.

Pozzuoli: the overcast day
streaming, uncertain and grey,
a flooded temple
and sulphurous fauna and fern
near Virgilio's Averne.

Cumae caved and rock-like.
Cumae of the hundred doors,
Cumae dry and deserted.
Cumae that no-one ignores.

Cumae with her English-Latin
and her English-Italian
and the drawing-crayon: why here?
Did the old sibyl hidden in Cumae
deride or revere her?

Cumae caved and rock-like,
of the hundred answers, dark.
How did she know that sola
forever she must work,
sola, attempting her art.

Gold Finishing

Scraps of gold left on the kitchen bar
and green leather parings are swept away
to clear space for our marmalade and toast. ˗
Across the room a set of volumes boast
their new ornate gilt labels – not my worst.
In morning light there's warmth from coffee first.
Omar Khayyam, his symmetrical capitals
outside in, waits gripped in the holder
beside the tumbler of wooden-handled tools,
whose slivers of many-times heated bronze
make words and letters and a wavy rule.
Gold finishing of books was invented for winter,
intended for times of darkness, so I know
that when I look outside the kitchen door
no leaf, but winter aconites all glow,
gold studs of material on green
part imagined, part crafted and part found
like Omar under Pogany's silvery moon.

Fishing in Gairloch

The three subjects of poetry are love, death and poetry.

Above the loch known as the aeroplane
the loch known as the diamond gleams all day.
Twin glinting lochans called the spectacles
are neatly pocketed behind the brae.

You think it isn't true? It's true.
Gairloch's the bit you'd hold the map of Britain by
high on your left, if your right hand steadied the lump
of Kent and Sussex below the Thames.
The map might break at the Thames, or it might break
across the narrow part of Northumberland.

You think nothing so beautiful
could ever happen inside this space,
a huge island you are sick of. We can fly out,
but we don't. It solves nothing. We come back
with another Greek dress, an Italian jug,
swatch of Aussie photos,
moon dust.

We can't have a new land, hence fiction.
Poetry is sworn to the truth
but it may take the road of fancy towards the truth.

How Dylan Thomas did it

In London among the mashed potato and poems in a studio
of Cardiff men speaking English and making girls plague
the smart Varsity editors of disgraceful rags,
owning, devouring letters between friends and fiancées
and the looming figure of threadbare Edith in London Paris
America. Seagulls crowd rudely, lorries brake, hot tarmac
melts the mirages of girls who write stories and stay middle-class.
He is Shakespeare in Swansea, Taliesin in London
but in America only a visiting twerp
poet with a drink problem and a musical voice.

American Emily and Sylvia

Always give or take a feminist change of ground,
an oligocracy, economic war fought in the home,
fought by scribbling mothers, workmen, pavement artists
local government officials, buskers, teachers, screamers
& people who would hide in a room and write.

Young women mopping babies – no playroom laptop
but scrubbed elm lid, a hermit window wide –
clashed words slip out, slide round, fly everywhere
to pool in poems, play tig with elves of night
and count their winnings in the quiet dawn.

How Gerard Manley Hopkins did it

I draw and pray with words, take sailships
from Liverpool to Clyde, through Scotland with Black's guide
back in the eighteen-sixties though you wouldn't credit
my boi-oi-oink rhythm and my general comments
with not being modern

Inversnaid, a remote waterfall low-to-lake-falling
on north east Lomond. The trees are inspired and make my poem.
After me many a nun woman or man poet possessed
of every one of my ordered ordained words yessed.

At this point *This darksome burn horseback brown*
is quoted, as much of it as the reader can remember.
Hopkins was still considering Mediaeval Moderns, Rossetti et al.
And he *desired to be where springs not fail* etc.
We can't talk about Hopkins outside his own words
and this is the ultimate accolade of a poet
but makes him not much use to the universities.

Rain falls on the lochan, the spongy everything
of heather, slate-blue blaeberry, butterwort, ling
stretching to screes and peaks; a few red deer
who can be dangerous at this time of year.

The poets in the North of England drain from the moorlands
and collect in a puddle in Huddersfield. The poets in London
sulk on the tube in the dwindling rush hour.
Plonking words together, necessarily other people's
used words, is this an honourable occupation
to which we are driven, habit to mad pastime?

Why not sit by the loch and fish,
why not sit by the loch and wish.
Rain patters on your black umbrella
while the sun shines on the other fella.
Why, because fish skulk in the cool dark stones,
alive, apart in fathoms, of irrevocably distant intellect,
but I do not wish to kill them. Political correctness
has very little to do with it, their deliciousness
has less. I am a soft creature in some ways
but not when it comes to sorting out a poem.

It is ideas I fish for, here in Gairloch
ideas that I invite to my beautiful home.

How Keats did it

Shakespeare wore out many pens, tools of necessity,
gleaned twenty-five years harvest, twenty years
not wasted, central in England, central in time.
Keats' pen, further on in history
rushes on mischief, meshes his short years
of sedged precipices far too visibly.
La Belle Dame hounds him mercilessly.
In Highgate's enchanted forests, chases of Enfield,
Now more than ever seems it rich to die.
He made illness help him. I don't resent Keats' death.
I have always resented Dylan Thomas' death .
Dylan Thomas was a fireball. Keats was a moonbeam.
Both of them loved women. Isabella staring at her basil-pot
flowering from the skull of her lover. Caitlin with ice-cream
on her arm, asking her dinner-party neighbour to lick it off.
Caitlin wrote poetry in secret. There is always a lover and a loved.

How Stevie Smith did it

North London again. Glenda Jackson
who is beautiful, socialist and professionally concerned
knows how to look a deliberate frump, protecting
so delicate a language machine
from invasion. Stevie, thankful to be at last dead,
peeps over a cloud-edge, approving of Glenda's
political support.

To the beautiful green brae in the view of the sea,
flooding pale earth with the witchery of thought,
the aeroplane takes us along, but it cannot land.
To collect for Chicago requires three miles of flat land,
a crew of six, a battalion on the ground.
A journey beyond the moon is impracticable.
But a journey to Gairloch is just about feasible,
the god of the motor road more or less pleasable.

Language is driven west
and comes back east like birds,
driven west by history
and brought back east by spirit.
Westerners, Irish and Celts,
from Easter Island and Holyhead, Gairloch and Ireland
they come to Paris, to Stratford, to London,
from Chicago to Edinburgh.

Winged pilgrims, fat gulls, sea-parrots
and the swift-flying field birds, all come in,
arrive in all directions towards the sun,
which never stops rising, only colouring clouds
before it comes up again.

The braes of Gairloch scorch. Hamlets huddled
against the lee of cliffs receive their shade.
The sea, normally death-cold, swelters.
No sea- or land-mist is distilled or made.
London lies in a hotter than ordinary summer
but Scotland, Scotland is warming up. No longer
is there a temperature difference between Newcastle and Leeds.
Newcastle is like Napoli, Edimbourgo is like Rome.

Brick-gold clouds of leaf
releasing twig lattice
the birch tree season gets shorter.
Huge purple jellyfish pile round the coast.
In Gairloch we live with our remoteness,
far along slow roads, safe from change,
our loneliness guarded by passing places,
wild loops of road with mountains in them,
tides and unbridgeable lochs.

Petrol changed Gairloch a little,
        but the passing places smile.
The demon change we fear.
        We retreat to the cool
undamaged hills. Our chilly scene
        shall last.
We need to distinguish
        the future from the past.

        Are there clouds in the sky
                bringing threats in the air
        to the structure of an atom
                and the ozone layer?
        Is it true what they say
                that our world, never led
        simply zooms on its way
                through a hole into space
        with a god giving chase
                like a ray through the ice,
        (maybe ultra violet maybe infra red)
                dangling into darkness with a fishing rod?

And yet, there is a hole. For people know
  that in and out of life, signs come and go.
    Dear love, beloved death
      sing with their unworldly breath.
        Secret places like the moors,
          no streets, no people, out of doors
the indescribable towns of tadpoles and jellyfish,
  tadpoles in freshwater, jellyfish in the brine,
    from the secret places come voices,
      of singers who thinly aspire
        to find similar voices,
          to join in a choir.

When the bruise-blue, the blackberry-blue sky
brought rain the colour of the making of the highlands,
set dancing the fresh water, drove to fury the salt wave,
we all praised every goddess we could think of.
We needed the rain for the crops and for our dry hearts,
water for the animals and to cook with,
and to refresh us so we could properly think,
and to turn milk powder to milk and ink powder to ink.
Hot sunshine is all very pretty in Rome or Africa
but with twenty hours' daylight we can't take heat as well.

Now, though, the hell is over, the birches drink, ships
schooners and galleons lurch forward, their sails
flapping wet and happily in the hopeful weather
while sea-loch and inland loch reduce their yards of silt,
the tide rising at sea and the rainfall raising the deep
of the monstered pool, the river in its steep banks.
How McGonagal did it. He told things as he saw them
and he went *plink* at the end of nearly every line,
which, in poets who are not thought ridiculous,
is referred to as rhyme.

McGonagal was as crazy as Cowper and Clare,
as Edinburgh's Fergusson. But who from the North was there
Where were the Northerners? Where were the women?
Who represented our singing hearts? Our sighing souls?
Who sang our slogans, calling, Come to the Sun?
Lonsdale in Moonlight? Poetry Huddersfield?

Wordsworth and Dorothy walk.
They sleep standing up that pair, looking out on
the simple north. Dorothy keeps silence
for her brother, a scribe for blindness
to womankind, *poor Susan, Behold her Singing.*
Cambridge calls northern scholars. Wordsworth writes.
The Rev. Patrick Brunty writes.
We talked funny and dressed funny.
Ideas, like wine, don't always travel.

Three lochs.
An aeroplane, to escape in.
A diamond, to wonder at.
And spectacles, for vision.

This time of year the deer are dangerous
so we have left our poet from Chicago
staying and writing in our home in Edinburgh
or at the table she's reserved in Bewley's
(the Irish cafe) talking to a friend
and wondering how we're getting on in Gairloch.

We said we'd like to take her out of Edinburgh
and show her Scotland in the raw, a dangerous
excursion to the sea-lochs, far from Bewley's
and let her feel the poetry of Gairloch
remote, unpeopled, quite unlike Chicago,
but she preferred our city with a friend.

We talked before and after of Chicago,
which she observed was socially like Edinburgh,
and neither city did she think as dangerous
as hillsides filled with snakes and deer. A friend
looked after her while we went off to Gairloch.
The pair of them sat writing poems in Bewley's.

So she sat fishing for ideas in Bewley's
while we were fishing, selling books in Gairloch,
the book that she was signing for a friend,
which we had lately published here in Edinburgh.
The great stag, daring enterprise, so dangerous,
roamed fabled hills, oblivious of Chicago.

These tiny lochans, dots on maps, my friends,
reflect here while you recollect at Bewleys,
the great loch, deep Maree still guarding Gairloch
named from Mulrubha, known of in Chicago
as older than the other myths. In Edinburgh
the mist-clung precipice of thought is dangerous.

Love, death and poetry. We found in Gairloch
peace, words and wilderness, while you, our friend
had planned a meeting next year in Chicago.
Crowds, cities, airports, traffic, dangerous
hillsides of civilization, meet in Bewleys
(just like in Dublin). Farewell, Edinburgh.

Joke (traditional)

Spill a pint of beer in Dublin
    / Edinburgh
    / Huddersfield
    / Chicago
and you drown ten poets.
Drop a breadcrust in Gairloch
    / aeroplane
    / diamond
    / spectacles
and you feed 1,000 tadpoles.

The Rivers

In season those ungainly clowns
  hop round the peaty logs
till longer and more sightly leaps
  declare them poet-frogs.
In a land of lochs not of rivers,
  green and silver in hue,
the shortest river in Scotland
  runs for a mile or two.
It links land-loch and sea-loch
  and somewhere at its side
is an unimportant river
  that isn't very wide.
The small one's called the Kerry
  and the short one's called the Ewe
for where you get one river
  there are very often two.
(Thus the persuasive power of verse
  sanctions what isn't true).

The Poets' Pubs

In season these ungainly clowns
hop round the wooden chairs
and scramble for the jugs of beer
like a troop of greedy bears.
In a world of words and meanings
of images and song
the longest river in Britain
runs on and on and on.
It was mentioned in old Dublin
by Parisian James Joyce
It was named in the Mabinogion
in a very ancient voice
but to all of us, the moderns,
who are borne by its tide
it is nameless, wet and terrible
because we are right inside.
(So we sit inside our poets' pubs
swallowing our beer and pride.)

I took a train to Huddersfield
and met them on the station,
the shuttle flight from hell descended,
poets of the nation,
the airliner from USA,
the bubble-car from Wales,
the sophisticated Londoner
who had hitched a lift in a Jaguar.

From Whitby, Leeds and Manchester,
from Dublin, Howth and Edinburgh
led roads and routes to Huddersfield
and we gathered on the way,
a motley group of sojourners
like those in Chaucer's day,
pundits and pardoners
and verbal gardeners.

Where have you come from?
Chicago? London? Kent?
from solitude or city streets,
and is what you meant
by *aeroplane, diamond* and *spectacles*
escape, wonder, vision
or death, love and poetry,
or love, poetry and death,
or poetry, love and no death?

The hills, roads, seas, lochs, rivers of Gairloch
sink into the night. Diamonds of passing places
grow luminous in the shaky darkness.
Cars visible by battery headlight dive towards cottages,
sparse bothies and crofts. Spectacles are useless,
the book is an open world. Binoculars sight dark craft,
eagles. Keen fishermen trek back
to the licensing hotel. Tourists with woollens.
Sheep sitting on the road, counting cars.
They can count up to three.
Aeroplanes keep away. It's dangerous.
We sleep here. Our poet thinks of us in Bewley's.

Newcastle is crammed with initiates
and bearing claret out of Windsor come
the Yorkshire boys. Airliners circle and queue
to land on three-mile strips.
North London, Dublin, Paris, Wales.
Scandinavian and Scot with the strength of the long hills,
excitable Latins and Welshmen.
Poetry is of language and of journeys,
by boat, horse, road and motorway
and by aeroplane.

Rivers. Lochans. Hopkins. Dylan Thomas.

Dylan Thomas is dead.
He has found a pleasantly warm bank in hell,
where he sits joking with a few old whores.
His black T-shirt says
in red letters, *Dracula in the Vernacular*.

Gerard Hopkins is dead.
He has volunteered to take prep in purgatory.
He is writing out, *I must not waste time at Waterfalls*
thousands of times, and sinning at his task.

And Stevie Smith said, *It is the very bewitching
hour of eight*, in Hendecasyllables.
I love to hear the pretty clock striking eight.
Stevie's Hendecasyllables should now be recited,
as much of it as anyone can remember.
But it isn't in her books.
She put it in a newspaper. The besom!
Both and also because waking up ends dreams.

Keats

I ran away to Scotland, the people for to see...
but I'll have to write much better for immortality.
There's my brilliant Hyperion, my tacky Agnes' Eve,
so more of the splendiferous, O Muse, may I receive.

I am in India. I am in Arabia,
a red rose grows on my grave.

I choose wine.
I choose idyllic country life.

Fitzgerald sings of me.
I come to London and make my own English.

Come now, Sweetie, the youth says to the buffalo
(on the Strip of Herbage).

I come from the past.
I bring jewels from the north-west monasteries,
Welsh gold, pearls from the rivers.
I bring the rhyme of France,
ballads of the Troubadours,
the chivalry of ferocious Crusaders.
I have to bring them somewhere and I bring them here.
How Tagore did it. How Omar Khayyam and Fitzgerald
did it.

Wake up, said a soft furry animal, wake up.
You are in white-hutted, green, misty,
west-country-rainy Gairloch,
fishing for ideas.

The Arrivals

Every hot summer morning there are poems
all over the inside of the computer.
Was it me that put them there
in the amnesic lethal moonlight of the dark,
emergency lighting of the common stair?

The fountain pen's soft cylinder
controls its inner mechanism, simple
as the stunning invention that writes down,
the uncontrollable by the artless, the words
the god of music gives; we learn.

Or rubbing from the leaden graphite
in softwood pencil shavings, ringed
with fine red or yellow or blue flaky paint,
onto the roughish paper, half-inch lined
parade shiny-buttoned more of the same,

bunching themselves into battalions
of four, five, six or fourteen lines,
suicide warriors eight or twelve abreast,
two weak to every strong, pirouetting
like foxtrot footsteps on a primer page.

I preen the verses, do not detonate their bombs.
I just come and comb out their beauty,
brush down their uniforms. Pray, do not
blame or praise me for the poems; history
comes from sources, not from historians.

Yew Hedge

The smallest seedling admitting to be a yew,
patterned leaf-spines striking from a mashed berry
of poisonous progenitive orange dye,
and the youngest oakling disillusionedly staring
at three hundred years' work, envy the rampant vine
bolting up the yard fence, snatching a telegraph pole
out of its asphalt forest floor, corkscrew tendrils
wanting to grab and defend everything, dragonlike
bacteria, slow dragons, a hayloft,
cornflowers and poppies withering in the scented grass,
everything, horses and wheeled horsepower, ideas
and their eccentric propounders, books, rocks,
wavy seaweed, auctionloads of paraphernalia,
gravestones and photographs of gravestones, images
of preChristianity preserved about a village cross,
a grey church magically screened by edifice of bush.

But work is work
and yew will grow
by being planted
in a row
a trained eye
lightly wielded clippers
a good site,
good digging,
good neighbours.

How black it is in the bark of the yew. How firmly
the thickset herringbone of twigs and leaves restrains
every passing arrand and scuttling curled tan leaf
of the clean oak with its airy pits and ridges
un-dustspecked even to the ordered grooves of the fruitcup.
The black dirt is in the nature of the yew;
it collects old words like arrand meaning spider,
each on a wandering errand into the end of history,
up the bough that was lopped for bow-wood so long ago,
the wound so far past weeping as to be invisible,
down the roots that yearly thicken under the tulip bulbs,
know that cluster to thrust through delayed wintersnow,
sending their exotic rondels to clash with the mossed shade,
benefiting in light from the trees' lateness of leaf,
floor-planting part of the whole yew experience, yew-ness,
the cosmos yew with hardy nests, bright ladybird beetles,
the skeletons of the deciduous, white as poplar,
halted for ever like prehistoric bones
sightless in their lugubrious canopies.

> but life is life
> and work is work
> and yew will grow
> it will not shirk,
> will not grow high
> till it's grown low
> and all it asks
> is no changed minds
> for twenty years or so.

Dublin, 1963

I loved it then and still remember
the way the city let me wander there,
the smelly Liffey and the drollery
by colonnade and bridge, establishment and square.
Embellished richness, unperturbed by poverty.
A true appreciation of Dublin
came to me early. Not yet ready
for people individually, I had come
alone and drawn, to trudge the pavement,
wondered at by the lady of the cheap hotel
but not wondered at by the old men of the pubs,
who had often seen young writers
who did not yet know themselves
but recognised the city's literary power.

Visitors

Yes, they were desperate decisions
and they began tentatively:
as, *this sounds like poetry;*
I think I shall go away.

They were the ends of arguments
that followed visitations
I instantly recognised
though absent so many years:
aged and changed by age
yet shockingly familiar:
old love and the muse.

Why did they come to me,
spectres in silk and gold?
I have not forgotten them.

Despair!

Oh, Horace, what should I do?
These have been in a drawer ten years
and they are still not poetry!

Five Time Poems

Tomorrow

Today the sea with its red-strip tarmac prom,
brown-gold stone lit by evening, clean blue water,
seems very very old. The sand-playing young,
clad in scant memories as they hop and run,
imitate rock-fauna. Thus they make this strand
their day's universe, decorate it, use it, knowing
only that it will be replenished tomorrow, like youth
itself. Viewing their knowledge, from this stance
that took long climbs to gain, although I never knew
exactly where it poised at any given cue,
I sense my mind has shed skin, abdicated shells,
greater and metamorphosed, hung on thread
of self existence, still holds, but to what sandcastle
rampart or unknown wave-front could I aim?
Did I consider the first split bivalve, cockle shells
I'd click together again with fingers
that had touched so little? Did I not fear
dune and scavenger and wave when I was young,
younger than I ever remember being,
just as I now never remember being as old
as at moments when I look on time itself, or what is young,
or what has stood forever or occurred again, again
as the tide plays its jokeless game again, again
and girls' daughters and sons usurp the height
and purpose of their disadvantaged parents.
Yet I am not decrepit. Life is long
as the sea surrenders to the gold wall again.

Life is not even repetitive. It slurries round
changing consistency and always looking different,
coloured pebbles left in patterns and rows after the tide
or moving arrows of the estuary birds
chasing low-life prey in yellow-weeded mud.

38

What we do notice is repetition,
an exactitude returned, as on this present day
when cliff breezes come prancing back from years ago
and bring people with them who cannot return,
attitudes and beatitudes we never should see again,
specific happiness of water, sand and hope
gelled and held, a new production from a recipe.
Today the sea. Yesterday the cornfields. Tomorrow the sky.

———

Tomorrow cannot be the same as yesterday
so why does one warm afternoon yet seem
to match another? Why are these flowers those bouquets
set out on a student's desk that fluttered so long past
to philosophy, intuition and inspirational bombast,
imagination, sexual imagery and nonsense?

In any order those flowers and flower-thoughts
look out from *these* flowers, float though they may
in a wall of scythe-length green, creative rain
to so rock time even in my unimportant brain,
although it counts in that I'm doing the talking
and no-one can interrupt whatever I say
till I choose to let a breath into my musings
which obviously I shall have to do eventually
(else I shall be accused of cleverness,
one of the great sins of art, more horrible
than thinking it easy or using an old-fashioned rhyme scheme).
OK so God implies some sort of time scheme
but would a time scheme hang around for God?

What would the seven days of creation look like in the future?
How would anyone know there would be seven of them?
Let's work it out for ourselves, one for the seas,
one for the trees, one for the insects, ants and bees,
one for non-swimmers marooned on the ark,
that's five, and one for light and dark, that's six.
Then stop. Imagination's easily exhausted.
Shall we make Loch Ness Monsters, or just the idea of them?
Shall we make TV adverts and little green men?

Six days to make the world, and the seventh
looks like the first day of the rest of time,
not a rest, not one miserable day off to do the housework
before a return to the rush hour millgrist
nor a paid eight and a half hours off the clock
but just, pack it in. Tired of making the world.
Clear off leaving the shopfloor covered
with blunt blades, shavings and bits of thread.
I'm off to San Tropez for the ice-cream licence
on the topless beach. Off to Hudson's Bay
to stop the fur trade. Ride bareback on a porpoise.
Seek romance in the inadequate world I made.
Let the world get on with itself (and it did).

Nobody could be very good at it,
making worlds. I owe this thought
to Miroslav Holub, whom I am not supposed to quote.
I can also infer it from pissed-off politicians, who tried
in their different way. And from animals
that became extinct. Or lost their innocence, or died.
Or being innocent were unable to recognize it,
as the uncritical or colourblind
never know what they have missed.

———

The green of this summer is monochrome.
Watering all these leaves in drought
I would not recognise the lamina as green,
merely a bright-dark colour; black-and-white
and the rainbow I would have to do without.
The green of this summer is a curtain,
a dream, a mysterious prison,
a playground with no way out,
and the experience of being inside it
is what we call consciousness,
what we call 'I'. That is why I
am an agent in my own experience,

and why I assume that you, dry late lilies,
and you, crooked incongruous coltsfoot-leaves
to which only a botanist would gesticulate,
hang about listening, deliberating on a green summer
made from this prisonlike state.

A treatise on green is a distraction
like a number of very pretty doodles
on paper on which one is trying to write.
The doodles are rhythmic and have a pattern,
they strengthen and vary, they have verses.
They go right round the edge of the paper
like a letterpress border, and join up
all in the one handwriting. Doodles have heartbeats,
they are an expression of time,
as if the hand wrote automatically all the time
the heart beat its life out. 'Being a writer'
sometimes feels like that. The heartbeat.
The footfall. Eliot echoing in the memory, perhaps.

Time isn't like you or me being late for something,
nor is it the property of a very clever man in Cambridge.
Nor is it the peep-peep-peep of a funny alarm clock,
nor even is it the end of an old man's life.
There are a million things time is not.

And yet, time is very stark. It is what prevents me
from having tea with Charlotte; from going to a lecture by
Blake.
From taking part in a play by Aristophanes, a premier in
Greek.
It prevents me from reading the literature of the 22nd century
or from even having the faintest idea what it will hold.
If I am not on the right spaceship, I've had it.
I think on a small ship, somewhere remote, with timetables.
I am in a green garden. You are here.
The seaside, the sky and the cornfields.
Tomorrow.

Forget

[towards a statement about poetry]

1

The Ted Hughes, Tom Gunn 'firsts' when I was twenty,
following rapidly from Eliot, yellow Faber poetry,
forget the single pamphlet *Four Quartets*,
devoured in York or anywhere I could get them,
forget the Caedmon voice of Dylan Thomas
& remember being young and in a garden
and remember Auden underneath a quince tree,
a starling and a willow wren
and the wrinkled face in the Sunday papers.

2

Forget the poetry conference in London,
forget the other girls, all Poets' Women,
the poets all students, like Zulfikar Ghose,
and someone who I thought was William Plomer
(but might have been my friend Sebastian's father)
and remember Stevie Smith with her faint wailing,
her crossness when I spoke to her
(to her I did speak), and remember
it is the very bewitching hour of eight...

3

Forget rejection slips from Howard Sergeant,
later, long letters recommending yeast,
forget the loneliness, forget the silence
and how life filled up the waste with its own feast;
remember country buses, Wordsworth's Ode,
and *The King Sits in Dunfermline Town*, in schoolrooms,
and remember the sudden incongruous shock of Hopkins,
when, when, peace, will you, peace.

4

Forget school holidays and term vacations,
the work, the food, the lectures, the black robe,
remember the silky sunlight, remember the velvet twilight,
remember Virgil, Horace, in the Loeb.
Remember the words of the Greeks, the speeches that
Sophocles speaks,
the Shakespeare plays (forget the Globe clang-rhyme)
and think of the walks we took up Cheviot.
Remember the great lines, all the time.

5

Forget, if you can, Rome Paris Turin London,
– they're much too important to forget,
and the artists poets and writers who peopled them
(and future poets who haven't written yet).
Forget about dear old Betjeman and Pam.
When sudden Wham
MacDiarmid Soutar Henryson Davidson
Garioch Burns Norman Sorley
Scotland's voices, where I am

6

To remember Naomi Mitchison, 97, up the Argyll coast
with 6 women writers 2 gardeners
4 secretaries and a BBC outside broadcast.
I am a woman and remember only men
except for Stevie, aforementioned; how the great sun
set gold on Empress Edith in the west,
Sylvia daring, and, famous in failure, dead –
the lave unpublished, unimproved, unread –
Sappho a pitiless pitfall. Akmatova, and last,
Emily Dickinson calling over the dark water.

7

Forget the feminist heritage, poetry and babies,
the many organized readings in the pubs,
meetings, trials accidental and contrived,
the arguments and cliques the Muse allowed
or was not given a ticket to; the language
("old people and children may be present"),
the churchoes and politicos intruding,
and then remember a true love affair
and someone saying, *Make a quantum leap,*
write enormously better. It's the way.

8

And after years and years and years of reading
till varied writers partied in my mind,
and after innumerable screeds of writing,
the favourite lines they and I sometimes found.
The musical silences behind those lines,
as the tongue-loosened women cursed
(or my favourite colleague men tried to mend
recreate or regenerate word-worlds)
Language's need as it rocks to a sunburst.

9

Ah should I quote from them for a last word
as toward the distant, helpless flat-earth end
we speed on, they and I; some have already gone
splooshing and caressed, into the pothole-waterflume
of the wonderful underworld of the ancients
– they do not walk beneath their rotting bones.
Or instance from my dearest modern friends
in the pen the syllable and the boundary
the last links from a forge in a foundry?
The metalwork is not yet cool enough to build
a causeway, and the chasm can't be filled.

Here in the Study

Here, in the study inside the mind
similarly shelved with memories
in loaded pages and emphatic lines,
or the unsaid in white rivers of space
like rapid water over purling stones –
is it the water or the stones that sing,
is it the shape round the edges of letters
or the hard imprint in itself we read,

fight the undertow with several senses
till its music sings in our head,
takes an easy-chair in that soul-hall
and wonders which glossy or gold book it will open,
those marked with the dates of years
those with the names of the loved dead,
precious, poetic, assumed, accepted screeds,

Wordsworths and Tennysons of our private life,
Pindars and Swinburnes of our sorrows,
banalities and impossible complexities
postcards with five words allowed in greeting,
and three-volume blockbusters, inconclusive.

We write to breathe and breathe to write,
we whom every god maddens,
cast down, caught up, watched like windowpane
spiders and raindrop flies, has saddened
with shootings and mountain-swallowings, sudden death
arising like rhyme unbidden, a final knife
in the soul's determination to run its own life,
and whom the same gods afterwards have spared
(sparing is always a god's doing) have gladdened.

Enough of these short-syllabled big mysteries,
gee-oh-dee's, the ultimate and simple,
hardly mysterious at all to the childlike and wise,
children up trees, beldames boiling kettles
of fairly pure water for innocent herb teas,
congregated crones and wrinklies with tobacco pipes,
and nothing else to say till tomorrow.

When you press some wrong button
on a computer, as all have done,
the lines spring down the pages
out of step with each other,
quotations bunch themselves in the wrong place,
commenting, with the wrong emphases,
inapposite things to each other.

The computer seems to behave as if it had brains!
This I do to the world: I won't have
this history, I say, as if the world were a child
and I wiser. I am not wiser than the world.
Yet I dictate to it my wish: I flick switches,
seek solitude, carefully select companions:
some would say God does likewise.

What I see is a game I will not play.
I'll prepare tea and tease in the pavilion,
noting only the old Shakespeare adage
Will not and Cannot are related by the mind
and vastly affect metaphysics.
The minute I Will Not, I am in control,
though the state of play be indeed I Cannot.

There is always a lot of I in thought,
especially in thought inside a mind.
What would thought outside a mind be like?
Would it be the reality of a made page,
perfection of a blood-black paeony
or ghost-white lily against the green
that camouflages all fertility? Unless,
for instance, fertility were yellow or gold
and barren deserts kind as well as beautiful.

Unless daisies could really be our silver
and buttercups our gold for rule, impressing
our power, not merely a fob to peasant kids
whose urban gleams, jaguars our delight
policed pageants our inheritance, are known:
we only get daisies buttercups and guns
that's our dole, we must take, take by working
or take by impressing with tinplate and talk.

Give, give: taking will come of its own accord.
For all these strategies assume
the unproved premise that fate has logic to it.
Our route is steep, rivers too wide,
our horses weary before the end of it,
and come the shore who shall design a boat
or find available timber that will float?
Logic can't come with us. Confused, we seem
creatures of fate but creatures who can dream.

Memory

Memory is an empty line,
memory spilled like a glass of wine
red as redcurrants, green as oak,
white, white as the golden dawn,
empty and inconsequential, unwritten blank
pages or lines that lack, do not yet have a rhyme
in the original unity that is beyond time,
where only on the step of one statement
is another possible (let alone sublime)
the number of lines in a stanza is undecided
by the poet, it will be *abbastanza*
but for all we know irregular; the poet
has not proved herself or himself and might thank
himself or herself to stop, like I did.

Be new and sparkling, memory, like my friends
my parties plans and poems are, might they be
ah but what we intend and what we indent
are often dismally different; my critics
who are also my friends, old paralytics
and maniacs of the pen, one recorder
wired up to experience and producing results
which are not desultory, then divining
a pattern in the results: constructing history.
Without memory there is no eternal mystery.
Without mystery there is no life-interest
to differentiate between areas of the forest.
Without a forest there is nobbut a dry plain
and without leaves hardly any point in any rain.

Memory is a kind of life but it is not life
as these fourteen line stanzas are not sonnets
because sonnets are round. Sonnets are self-completing
while memory is for ever and ever meeting
itself in a hall of mirrors, silvered and sham
creating myriad pictures of the one being I really am –
up at five o'clock of a summer morning
writing on the computer, with the back door locked
and a green thunderstorm dead all over the garden
in the form of wetness on the grass and flowers
that had grown hot lush and unwatered for many days.
Now their perfume is released all over the garden
and boring old muggins is writing time away
as though nothing will ever need to be remembered again.

Perhaps that's what we're all after, the end of memory –
that we will certainly achieve. But is achievement
always success, that is this question overhanging
this early-morning experience and clanging
like the milkman's or the postman's bell
saying Morning is come, another acre of time
fenced by temporary darkness. Hark, hark.
Geese cross the skywaste, cackling, the hollow
unnerving sound of travelling geese,
at dawn where a woman's face is unlucky, perhaps
as the chaps plod off to scaffolding or coalface
in what has come to be thought of as the ideal
industrial elysium, now it no longer pertains –
we have doubted its certain horrors and lost its gains.

We are left with tundras of memory and no map,
we try to trace back the watercourses, we try
to be debriefed by nobody, we know it was heady
but we cannot collect up words enough to pin it.
It is a great bowl and we do not know what was in it,
ghosts without substance and therefore without proof.
Even if there were such a snooty thing as proof,
we discover smartly that anyone can choose
not to accept as proof, any proof they might not wish
to give the name proof to. Proof is a trick,
besides not sounding kosher, not standing
repetition too well. There is only persuasion.
Persuasion is history, always at the ready
to deal with memory at her caprice.

Meanwhile, Memory, shall we have some peace,
seeing we are so trapped, let's ignore them,
and have our little tea-party, you and I,
on a gardened lawn; jasmine and gunpowder
and some conversation. We had a laugh,
oh yes we had a laugh. We loved
the countryside, and each other,
and we sailed seas, I think we sailed seas,
and we were rescued, yes we must have been rescued
for we are alive and well, if not yet any given age,
and there is a little left of today's sun, circling
in the gaze of our unity. Beauty here is seated
at a painted cloth, in forgetful mood,
and I, my dear, will not be cheated.

Oh Give Me Dreams Any Day

They speak again, like youth and daisies,
rise like religions and subside like dough
left too long, before the baking.
They catch people who are busy putting up
d-i-y extensions or demolishing
caved-in sheds. They are dreams
and memories of dreams.

I say I dreamed you were in the driving seat
and I grasped the handbrake as we careered
down the steep summer driveway in our little car.
Dreams never obey miles, or commandments.
We are their speciality. In our own garden
I look up through one birch tree summer-green
of systematic leaf and see a forest.

I call the corner by the fence a wood,
a hide where chicory-flowered artichokes
rise *en masse* with all their clones,
and dog-rose creeps out sideways for some air.
The wood is a cheat but a good cheat –
I never go so far as to call it a forest
but hedgehog and passing fox are there,
tomtit, fickle flocks of family bluetits,
and under all the humus, brittle bones,
and in the jungle treetops, butterflies.

Memory, our tea-party is arranged here
as promised, on a forecast day,
clouds passing deliberately like freeway cars,
and an empty, shady house, protecting
the garden's quasi-silence, half-life, whole dream.
Memory, I am a little delirious,
a silly old lady by a basket-table
talking to no one in particular.

See what the basket holds. Flowers! Scissors!
Secateurs! and chicken-wire, obeying
strange rules of twisted hexagonals,
necessarily, unobserved. Life goes on
like a quad with nobody about in it, no stuffy
or quirky professors, fluffy professors' secretaries,
clever professors' secretaries with an eye on the chair,
no-one, nothing like this, no one is there
but marooned vegetable life, a rife atmosphere
and me, though I don't count, sitting at a table.

I thought Memory was a Tragic Quean
but she turned up gay, dispensing juleps
with orange and mint in them
and pouring out anecdotes without stinting them.
I sat nodding and listening as she spoke,
aware how many jokes I was missing
but somehow, grateful for the rendezvous
and glad of her solipsistic *I-love-you*.

Dreams end how they like. But not poems,
which are not woken from. The fear
within the dream too great, or the alarm without
too loud, or the nonsense completed, all's done,
back into pleasing blackness the soul falls.
A broken poem's no good to anyone.

We ditch our broken poems, accept as made
only those that reach conclusions.
Perhaps we should value our unfinished poems
for their dreamlike qualities. Any that are finished
we should simply term *lectures* or *periods,* long sentences
of pedagogic intent, and egotistic intention.
A poem is a dastardly invention.

Oh give me dreams any day, they speak again
like youth and daisies,
rise like religions and subside like dough
left too long, before the baking.
They catch people who are busy putting up
d-i-y extensions or demolishing
caved-in sheds. They are dreams
and memories of dreams.

Basil's Land
for Basil Bunting

The gentle Northern tongue
travel took not from me,
the Scots would not look on,
southrons would sing wrong,
I heard in tree and dale,
beck and fell,
but only one
who used the sound well,
made notes drip from stone,
where Yorkshire is south,
Stainmore the backbone,
where high above a scree
a windswept tree looked out,
saw the scars of the sea,
forces, an estuary,
northern mid-light,
a vocabulary of vision,
solitude, delight.

Holy Island Castle Garden

Lutyens: Gertrude Jekyll –
can you make me a garden
for my castle above the sea?

Gertrude: Lutyens, I doubt it.
Your salt-marsh home
upon a rock
much impresses.
Fears of height,
that staircase,
raging wind and wave
hinder my visit.
I dare not leave
the castle I have climbed
where sea-thrift,
medieval wallflower,
and pagan daisy
cling unchallenged
to crevice, turf and rock.

Lutyens: Gertrude, let pilgrims
inspire your genius and skill
to match this refuge.

Gertrude: Haven-castle,
from your gallery,
eyrie courtyard,
west and east bedrooms
you shall greet my garden.
Down rock, across field
in sight and sound of sea,

Lutyens, I'll make you
a white stony growing place
cultured and sheltered,
safe as a siege
from the steep storms
of commerce, populace,
poverty and glut
beyond the tides
of the uneven sea.

Lutyens: I am an eagle and a sheep, Jekyll,
a merchant across the sands
come rich to pasture.

Memories at Lindisfarne

Unable to pass by the sign for Beal
I leave the main road, make for Lindisfarne.
My car negotiates the lane, the farm,
the level crossing then the causeway tides.
Here at the island's gate all history hides.
The road ends suddenly lacking a bridge.
If it's all watery, lapping grass and weeds
and rows of ugly silent concrete blocks
and hours till anyone can cross
then here is the most peaceful place on earth.

If it's nearly safe, sea pours away,
sand glistens, and an unassuming queue
of cars and pickups wait; a caravan
has pulled aside, where a southerner makes tea.
Saint and pilgrim also had to wait
and saint and pilgrim saw what she now sees
from her Formica tabletop. At dusk
or blazing morning, having travelled far
in snowtime or the season of the bee,
it's just another quarter-mile of sea.

You have to really want to come here.
Some come for religion , some for history.
The beer lorry brings barrels for the pub,
some come for holidays, some to paint or draw
who've never been here, or who love the sea,
and many come because they came before.
The locals head for Berwick or Newcastle,
or just the petrol pump at Beal; the bus
brings children home. Why, tide, pull me?
Orchids on beach-dunes, thrift on castle rock,
intimate flowerlets landlocked in memory,
rare, remote, travellers I came here with
whom now perhaps only the pilgrims see.

The Gap is the Poem

The old North Road   veers silently through Fife
this Sunday morning   farther than we walk
levelling the upheaval   of border miles
Edinburgh, Berwick   till it strides
to the Northern counties   roller coasts
and toughens Romans   for the Scottish hills
now littered   with the wept cross of wheels.
We think in snatches   ayes and legends.

In the cool clear weather   of how we talk
I see the whole distance   between old walls,
Antonine and Hadrian's   there from a southerly
no-go-country   to hair-raising mountains,
Carter Bar moor   and a Roman army:
viewing two hundred miles   of dips and fells,
doubling of danger and space,   unnameable land
giving its residents   a swordbearing hand.

This springtime   like sunlit Maypoles,
popular fairs   of runners in boaters,
fancy dressed kiddies   dressed in coloured crepe
fortune seekers   old candy swingboats
favourite fiddle tunes   and north of England songs
how could you leave me   here we come gathering,
a little straw hat   to set off the blue ribbons.
Charleses and Jameses   people the empty wall.

Bruises from Shrove Tuesday   football are gone.
Paste eggshell scraps   from the grassy hill
dyed in a kettle   with primroses and wool
bring us to the present.   All about us
(inside many of the houses)   Alex Kidd
or his advanced successors   plot their courses
through screens and shadows   of electronic chips.
The birds peep   through the historical leaves.

A rumour of a forced march   through the present,
modern Mithras and mistletoe   down by the river
a flat gateway fooled   by argument or claim
those Romans sent the lost   legion to Nijmegen,
inland Holland.   Inspired by gullies
our ravaged castles   our pale gold sands
rise from the sea   seek hinterland bolt-holes
in a green generation   of century gaps.

Hexham, Housesteads   and Sewingshields,
those safe hidden heights   whose revellers
paraded once-embittered   battle ground,
delved the approving grass   for telling trove.
Thin lilies,   all that will grow in Fife,
attend with eloquence   and silent trumpets
as myth beckons us   Scot and Englishwoman
our hair in ribbons and helmets.

To Robert Herrick

Your black future is come; I am he;
sound falls down merrily now merrily falls
by afternoon anticipating change;
by laneside whoops and whistles, designates
one prophet, good prophet who saw
dim christianity, dissemblance, lost peace-yen
and liking for a mystery
that is loving but not love.

Juliay your brown wife went
and lay long ago in turf;
coupled like pea and bean, oat and wort
the devil's winsomeness
touches us, still whole.
I have not found,
Robin, a better value for the fate-tossed,
rusticated, ageing,
limited or lively soul.

River at Oxford

Robin and I went down to watch the boats,
past the gabled houses, the straggling hops,
over an old allotment gate,
past the scout-hut, over the nettles and leaves,
onto a swaying jetty.

This, I said to Robin, is the land I left,
the land I barely knew, flat and wet,
warm and willowy. It goes all the way to London.
This is the river I was born by near Bow bells,
river of houseboat and trout and flashing oar.
Robin said nothing. After a while we padded on,
past the fruit trees and old man's beard,
hips and haws and blackberries,
I talking unnecessarily and Robin saying nothing.

Meeting Mandela

10.7.96 London

I saw Mandela in the Strand
as near to me as you now stand,
in a Royal Visitor's car
with motorbikes on every hand
        and agents everywhere.

I met Mandela for he smiled.
Welcome, Mandela! I went wild –
Great to see you! Very good!
as round me the policemen stood
        and no-one interfered.

The traffic was held up, perhaps.
It was a great security lapse.
The other Nelson just in view
I made friends with Mandela through
        the window of the car.

There's a world leader: here am I.
We both can smile, we both can cry,
and then the traffic moved again
and I went on, my head held high
        for I had met Mandela.

And as at last I moved along
I thought of Hamish Henderson
singing Free Mandela Free
Mandela as his opening song
        of every revelry.

He still sings Free Mandela though
the man is high up who was low,
and I'll tell Hamish Henderson
and everybody else I know
        I met Mandela.

Three Quasi-Sonnets to Writers

To Brenda Williams, Beseeching her to Write

Brenda, you can write like the wind
yet you stay mute as though you were
a plant with leaf and root, no flower
to expand into the hurricane
that makes those wooden shacks fall down
the other airs make breezes in.
Come out and set your verbs and nouns
and music notes in rowdier rows
through which like panpipes tremors flow
and use the fleshy leaf and root
to make substantial poetry
which, though so many may not hear
our silence will not serve at all.
With me come whisper, sing, shout, bawl.

To Angus for his Poetry

OK, you're drunk, and journalists get drunk,
it's your response to the international call,
where versifying might pull you through the bit.
It's happened often – but wait a minute,
you care for words and how they rise and fall,
you know the hallowed pages, have made friends
with Yeats, MacNeice and Auden and the rest.
Dylan Thomas would have trusted you,
and I trust Dylan Thomas. It's so sad that whisky
which offered health and life to our great Scots
saw Dylan off our needy world so quickly.
But we have age and years ahead of us,
a verbal buoyancy and we won't be sunk,
we're tough old steel that love and anger soften.

To Sorley Maclean

Over the cruel blue isolating water
signalling out to the unimpeded mountains
are thoughts patterned like constellations.
Sound carries their meanings on the ocean
in great sailing ships, Gaelic or English
as long as they are good ships, Sorley.
We ought all to be building a good ship
precisely because there aren't ever any bridges
in the muffling sand. Cloudlike she swings,
the beautiful vessel borne on the bard's wings.
Will we ever be afloat aboard the clipper,
her full sail astrodynamical in fair weather?
We know her for the delightfullest distant snow
plying between tomorrow and long ago.

Van Gogh's Sunflower in a Lothian Field

First Visit

Sunflowers among camomile and borage,
spread and patterned on a Van Gogh frame,
a field of folk-art, farmers' art, so strange
stared at by back-packers, making front-page news,
paparazzi and art students forming queues
by a path down the margin of fearful green,
shadow-blue, russets of hedgerows.
Sunbursts of foliage threaten to unhinge
the ragged acreage of apparent posy, foreign
geraniums, an anthology, porringer of fat fox-grass,
wheats, wild oat, purplish burdock, all your range
of old sandstones, colours you could scrounge
from arboreta, tigerlilies or tangerines –
a riotous fieldful of rhymes for orange.

Second Visit

How to translate this tortuous artist, crazed
by his brilliant eye, from the hot fulness of France,
his frilled language the colours of late romance,
his pointillism like the seeds of words
rushed into growth-swirls; how to make
his pictures into lowlands' give-and-take
of flat and formless pasturage? This mad try
by a boy down the dune-lands, echoes the essays
of the invincible brush, that wasn't, being French, Victorian.
It's not the nothing that ever happens, while I wonder
what turned this Jimmy into a Florian:
in the wierd edges of creativity where I wander
everything never happens at once.
Which *siècle* is this the *fin de*?

Ezra in Venice

The dry mist shrouding Ezra Pound
rises to show the grin of pain,
the fine phenomenon we found
once in a harsh historic reign.
Among Venetian byways pale
and rich but somehow fey and fake
on straits and wavelets see him sail
to forage concepts he could take
who owned so little as to say,
That which thou truly lov'st is thine.
Reliance on what is at last divine
unnerves us as we still pursue,
hunt through built cantos but he hides.
The biggest myth since Ulysses
on everlasting truth he glides.

Last Pre-Feminist Poem

I re-wrote other people's poems
as Lawrence rewrote Hardy's novels,
dipping the figures in another range
of colours, my language tangential,
my irrational numbers
small talk.
They did not say, 'Where were you educated?'.
"Have you got any money?',
or even, looking round my library, 'Your husband
must be intelligent.'

The absurd sound sense of these writers
so jolted my brain,
my heart (the measured pulse),
my soul (which may be others')
that I took them, at their level,
a reminder of Ruskin's word –
a man I could not have remained in a room with.

How, their introductory scribbles
derided by neighbour and wife,
did they intrude upon the cheerful party
I had set up and cooked for,
bring bluebells in, chuck stilted fucshia,
rip carnations from buttonholes,
exposing crumpled tinfoil,
a florist's wire distorting truth?

The party is ended abruptly,
guests spluttering in taxis,
keys fumbled for, a stench
of alcohol, cigar butt, traces
of canapés and broken glass.

All the refreshing morning I swept, aired,
washed and polished solitude,
promised it a sober partnership
and set my sights on daytime visions
after moonlit journeys, making accessible
at my elbow, Lawrence, poet and novelist,
Hardy, poet and novelist, Davies,
philosopher and tramp,
oldest and best of many sparkling friends,
recommending them to fortune
and a safer existence in my brain,
who enticed me
at their level

Dreamer, devourer, tramp,
philosopher, mother,
I am also self-healing
which was their secret.

Travelling

From river to river
through the undaisied grass
the road pushes from Ullapool
like a long chain of verses
linked in a story, driving
a rough wild epic in the remembered past,
this road, this day, and travelling here with me
people who inhabit only the mind.

From these fields and under this sky
we would have to invent heaven
which would not be difficult
under such a blue sky.
Heaven is Omar Khayyam's blue bowl
Keats' solemn nightingale singing
on Sorley Maclean's tree
in a night never darkening.

Eileen O'Leary's lament
soughs over the Western waters
and over centuries of hardship
hunting this sudden heaven
of warm green winds in a cold country,
fuel and fire under the sun
where so often clouds suddenly
shove Gravesian lyrics aside

to strike sunlight from relict bards
like fire from flint frightening
all the onlookers scattered round the slope
rocks and trees caves and wildcats,
all animaldom looking for poetry
as an answer, cushi cushi
Laura riding do not give up
your experiment, disheartened you are,

but see this bright shaft on behalf of
the everyone, we call it heaven
& streak in it with Dylan Thomas
before Auden's grateful fog.
I see you brought your anthology
from Ullapool with you, remarks
my unseen mentor. Yes I said,
this journey I am smuggling it to heaven.

Looking for Scotland

The rolling field
waved, brown over the bright
hedges. Her colander
burned with the fruit,
gooseberries, a few red,
to give a green jam
mixed with elderflower.
Brunton Turret
was not far away.
The white and brimming miles
of Roman Wall,
the North Tyne river.
How far away?
A mere ten years,
yet in those ten
how many muses
came and died?
Putting sugar to fruit
she still walks strong,
though her friends perished
and her friends' loves have gone.
She left the slopes
of black-ripe legend
for the feared country
it barred out.
Her friends' muses perished,
year upon year of jam
scattered with elder florets
were consumed like rhyme,
yet the memory of it
fell like fruit in time,
like bush and hedgerow fruit
she rolled, rich as the past,
rich as what perishes
into the bladed field
and does not come again,
no, does not come again
until the earth is worked
and stores of song may spring.

How nearly Northumberland was finding Scotland

I found Plashetts
ripe for rehousing along the railway,
birches and penny-buns
choice and inviting on the old alignment,
embankments and cuttings
water cowslips, water milkmaids,
ghosts of old waterlogged steam-routes.

I found Birdoswald,
Wark and Warden,
I followed the North Tyne, frozen –
walked up its hidden valley
snowscape with warm red wine,
and in the summer, redcurrants, gooseberries
to re-stock country wine.

I wandered in the wilds of Northumberland
looking for somewhere – Scotland I did not find,
not then. I found Powburn
a wide ring of suede-coloured champignons
keeping the shorn grass magic
for hundreds of years,
high air, lichens undisturbed
by man in van,
water, a shepherd's crook
small grey houses, an ancient look.

I found Kielder
filled with foresters' cottages
with children who never spoke to strangers
because there weren't any strangers,
Kielder high above a projected dam.
Kielder viaduct its feet in the dam
and higher, a Dangerous Field
adders bred.

I looked towards Corbridge,
and I saw a field of archaeologists
annual amongst the buttercups,
golden swaying grasses,
friendly brown soil and stones.

Stay inland, whispered the grass,
waving in the summer breeze,
do not go downvalley past Corbridge,
on to the Tyne for real, real coasters,
tall masted ships asail
through the jaws of the Tyne
to the harsh seas of the north,
the dull East English coastline,
Hartlepool, Hull, London.

Wait awhile, said the archaeologists
and listen to our tale.
We have a direct line to the past
in the buildings and stones,
magic of things that were used by savages!
I am looking for Scotland, I said,
have you a line to Scotland?
and I left them with many backward glances:
they looked so happy,
digging up graves, undoing time's ravages.

How could I know my search was for Scotland?
It must have been a search for where I came to.
How different from Northamptonshire
elm hedges thick with cow parsley and honey-
suckle and cousins in New Zealand and Australia?
The shoe-batterers did quite well for themselves
making Northamptonshire rich, yet the villages
at two-mile intervals reminded me
of those in County Durham.

In Newcastle I met
Basil Bunting and Hugh MacDiarmid
propping each other up
on the student society steps,
blind drunk on their way to the Poetry.
In those days you could drink and drive a point
as the young poets posed with young girls
practising posing as women
and the old poets posed with their adversaries
or plain posed.

Scotland is not that way, I said,
coming back from Northumberland
a hundredth time. Northumberland
is too like nowhere else to be near Scotland.

We took buses to Lindisfarne,
also got drunk, singing
O Sir Jasper and the Foggy Foggy Dew
stuck over on the tides,
too drunk to find the sea,
too drunk to be let loose on the causeway,
but perfect for walking the broad seaward beach,
of raised pebbles, the dunes
of lark and orchid,
on the religionless spur of land
lagooning northward.

How nearly the North was finding Scotland

The Lake District
I did not come back from:
forever beguiled by a magnet
strengthened at Penrith, encouraging
Keswick and Kendal, Ambleside
and southerly Kirkby Lonsdale.
At last the land spoke with the sky,
clouds slid down screes,
waters rose among meadows
and the land, never meant to be flat,
bent and created the sky dome
and the Lake District
was ever more a home.

But I had not found Scotland;
I went to the York Mystery Plays
in the good old days; sat on a platform
in a silk dress and watched pageants,
the whole of York being one:
I wrote in the Public Library
and in the massive museums
alone among fans and invitations,
alone among engines and inventions
performances and supplications.

How nearly Wales was finding Scotland

I went to Wales
and there I nearly found Scotland.
There I found mountains, tarns,
forests and philosophies,
a lisping church and raging languages.
The hills spoke, the rivers sang,
the birds appointed arch druids,
seas were everywhere, roads ran nowhere
(but mostly through Machynlleth).
and the threatening state of Blaenau Ffestiniog
and the threatening coal under the valleys
and the threatening atlantic waves
bashing the beaches and shattering sea-shells
where a small boat sneaks out for lobsters
and comes back with eels –
so nearly was Wales finding Scotland.

So nearly was Wales finding Scotland
that, up a slope of forest trees
over a tumbling watercourse
where squirrels hopped, a charcoal hut,
a river from which the distant hills
blue as the spiked Snowdon horseshoe
that might have been Cuillin
fooled me into thinking I was there,
& though a boy swam across a lake with me
it was places I loved, by which I was haunted,
places with which I wanted
to have the ultimate affair.

Not a night on a village hillside,
a castellated fortress above a grape plain
poplared like North Italy,
nor a stretch of cold empty Venice lido beach
nor a lush hunting forest in France,
filled with edible snails and freize du bois
and hot plants with stinking hairy names
nor a desert sandscape further south
familiar from television's pushy knowledge,
nor the vast continent the desert crowns
seen through a thousand travel books and novels.

Because yes, I did find Scotland at last.
I have to inform you, to place my bony hand
on your shoulder, or luggage, or drinks-tray
and make you listen, in the English
that is only perfectible here
or in other delectable country in the palm of a hand,
a pool in the palm, fingers for ridges
capable of grasping a mottled sky,
a clear blue night sky, or a black day-sky
under emotion's eclipse, a land
that can beckon sky, spill sky,
point, lift or delineate sky
or push firmly through sky like a tissue
pasted on a hoop,
to reality blinking in its self-begotten light.